3 THE HARD WAY

Overcoming Life's Obstacles & Making It Happen

JASON A. JONES

Copyright © 2025 Jason A. Jones

An Imprint of Journal Joy Publishers

All rights reserved and printed in the United States of America. No part of this book may be reproduced, distributed, or transmitted in any form or by any means, without the authors' prior written permission, except in the case of brief quotations embodied in critical reviews and specific other noncommercial uses permitted by copyright law.

For Publishing Information, contact Journal Joy at Info@thejournaljoy.com.

www.thejournaljoy.com

Editor: Nicole Gyimah

First Print Edition, 2025

BOOK DESCRIPTION:

"3 The Hard Way" is a memoir by Jason A. Jones, detailing his journey of overcoming life's challenges and embracing his unique identity. Born with a rare condition, Symbrachydactyly, which resulted in having only three fingers on his right hand, Jason shares his experiences growing up with a disability and how it shaped his resilience and determination.

Throughout the book, Jason recounts pivotal moments from his childhood, including his supportive family and the impact of sports in building his confidence. He describes facing societal perceptions and the struggle to fit in while maintaining his identity. Jason emphasizes the importance of resilience, patience, and the willingness to embrace change. He shares insights on the power of determination and the value of staying true to oneself while navigating life's uncertainties

Key Words: Resilience and Determination, Identify & Self Acceptance and Perseverance with Pursuing your Dreams | Self Help

FOREWORD
by Jonathan W. Jones

It is said that there are some people in life that make you laugh a little louder, smile a little bigger, and live a little better. Jason A. Jones has been that person for me throughout my entire life. He possesses an innate quality that makes everyone he meets feel like things will get better now that he has arrived. Luckily, the rest of the world now gets to know that feeling; because through this book, Jason has transferred that superpower into words on a page.

"3 the Hard Way" is an empowering body of work. It serves not only as a collection of Jason's most-valued memories; but also, as a summary of the crucial lessons he has learned from those experiences. He puts forth the story of his own life in order to weave a collection of hard-learned truths that one can only get from being a boy born with anatomical differences.

Life is hard - especially when you're different. But "3 the Hard Way" uses Jason's personal account to inspire all of us to embrace the things that set us apart, and harness our own uniqueness to rise above adversity. The knowledge that Jason imparts fits all audiences. But his message will strike a special tone for people who may have been born with "missing" body parts; those who have lost appendages due to accidents or illness; or veterans who have left literal pieces of themselves on the battlefield while serving our country.

Once you finish reading this book, you will undoubtedly know Jason better. And upon seeing the world from his vantage point, hopefully you will learn a bit more about yourself…

Anything is possible with determination, perseverance, patience, and the willingness to never quit. Although life is filled with obstacles and challenges that we are not always prepared for, we can accomplish anything that we intentionally put our minds to. There is nothing impossible for an individual who strives to be who they were created to be unapologetic.

This book aids parents that may have a kid with missing limbs, individuals who are down because of their current circumstances, or upset about how life has treated them so far. Throughout each chapter, I intend to encourage everyone that they can achieve anything with the right "Make It Happen" mindset despite setbacks and to overcome life's odds that every human being goes through, whether temporary or permanent. This memoir releases hope and encouragement to overcome past or present circumstances and setbacks that life brings by sharing some of my personal experiences.

Over the years, I've learned that life is full of twists and turns; peaks and valleys. Good things and bad things happen to all of us, but we must remember that life is filled with swift transitions, and things change daily; however, the only way to overcome them is to adjust and keep pushing forward. I hope by reading about my experiences, that it will help you start or continue the process of making things happen in your life, despite what you have experienced, are currently going through, or have faced the majority of your life.

This book reveals my strengths, my flaws, and my faith.

My situation is permanent but I choose to MAKE IT HAPPEN for me and not perceive it as an obstacle against me.

The choice is always yours!

CONTENTS

Part 1: Growing Up Different 1
- Chapter 1: Introduction 2
- Chapter 2: Building Resilience 6
- Chapter 3: Center Stage 21

Part 2: Facing Challenges 26
- Chapter 4: The Accident 27
- Chapter 5: One Step Forward, Two Steps Back 34
- Chapter 6: Odd Jobs, Big Dreams 38

Part 3: Embracing the Journey 45
- Chapter 7: Something Unexpected 46
- Chapter 8: A New Act 51
- Chapter 9: Recasting My Role 57
- Chapter 10: A Second Chance 62

Part 4: Break A Leg, Continue Anyway 66
- Chapter 11: The Power Within 67
- Chapter 12: You Can Make It Happen 78

Acknowledgements: 80

PART 1

GROWING UP DIFFERENT

Chapter 1
Introduction

No one ever comes to earth prepared for everything that happens. It's our first rodeo - all of us - and oftentimes, it becomes easier to give up hope than to stay the course.

Perhaps that's why I'm writing this story - this glimpse into a life that has turned out better than I ever saw coming despite my frailties, handicaps, and flaws.

I was born in a small town called Plainfield in Central New Jersey. My mother was a blessing (still is) with her uncanny way of reading my mind and her unusual ability to balance protectiveness with firmness as I grew. She remains one of the most significant influences in my life. Even though he was not always present, my father taught me enough to impact the man I am today.

I sometimes wonder how they felt when presented with the son they had been excitedly expecting. Were they surprised for a minute before embracing me and loving me with all their hearts?

Or, were they unfazed, dwelling only on the joy at the arrival of their son?

I think about this because I was born with a disability. A rare handicap named *Symbrachydactyly* meant I had only three fingers on my right hand. I have my thumb, middle finger, and index finger, with my pointer finger and pinky missing. It wasn't anybody's fault; there were no mistakes during pregnancy, and it wasn't something anyone could have predicted. Sometimes, life throws curveballs that no one can trace to any wrongdoing. However, it threw me my first curveball just as I came into the world.

Symbrachydactyly ((sim-BREAK-EE-DACK-til-EE) isn't a crippling disability. It is a medical condition where children are born with short fingers, which may be webbed or missing fingers.

It cannot be passed down via genes; it happens only once in thirty-two thousand occurrences, and most children born with it can do everything a normal child can do, as the child can get enough hand function with consistent treatment.

So, my condition wasn't a curse - especially since I had parents who never treated me like I needed special attention. They expected me to do what every other kid was doing, and I learned that I could always make my hand do whatever I wanted it to do. In retrospect, I greatly admire the fortitude it must have taken my mother to treat me the same, even when she watched me struggle. It must have taken a lot of guts to keep telling me I could do it, even when she wanted to take me into her arms and shield me from the world.

I grew up not knowing I had a "condition." My parents' love and the fact that I had been taught and encouraged to do everything that every other kid did made me feel normal - at least until I got out into the world and realized that other people saw the way I was born as abnormal.

My brother was born five years after I was born, and it was one of the most incredible experiences of my younger years. I had a brother who loved me unconditionally and was young enough to do everything with me. We had the most amazing childhood, content in sharing everything from babysitters to a similar love for learning.

I have a lot to be grateful for. It is the realization that as much as life throws its curveballs, it also finds ways to bring us the good stuff. For me, at the beginning of my life, the good stuff was my mother, who loved me and built a significant part of my resilient spirit, a younger brother who looked up to me like I was one of the most vital parts of his world, and a father who helped stir a love for the career path I eventually chose to pursue.

However, I can only see these things in retrospect. That's another reason I'm writing this story: to be that voice from the future who tells you it all turns out fine as long as you keep going.

From my experience, seeing anything good when the bad stuff is happening is quite hard. Perhaps, like me, you've wondered if there will ever be an end to the endless curveballs life chooses to throw or if it wouldn't be way easier to give up instead of trying to struggle through the complex paths of life.

I want to be the voice that tells you it is all worth it. I share my story, knowing that even if you have an entirely different story from mine, you still have to face challenges that are unique to you. And, even though I might not understand your specific challenge, I do understand what it means to feel different - like the only person in the room who has to deal with a problem that might never go away.

Chapter 2
Building Resilience

I didn't know what to say the first time my brother asked me why my hand didn't look like his. Shrugging while saying, "It just doesn't." seemed insufficient, and the curiosity splattered all over his face told me a one-sentence answer wouldn't cut it.

I settled for an answer that I found still applies today. I took him to the mirror, and as we stood together looking at our reflections, I asked him if we looked the same. At his vigorous head shake, saying, "No," I turned to him and asked him, "How come?"

He didn't know the answer, but the answer was that our hands couldn't look alike, just like we didn't look alike. Because, in retrospect, why is it okay for our faces to be different but not our hands, challenges, or stories?

That answer satisfied his young boy's curiosity until he grew up enough to understand why my right hand had three fingers while his and every other person we knew had five.

The answer I gave him was one my mother had given me the first time I came from elementary school, wondering why my hands were so different from the others. "This is the way God made you" and, even though it didn't give me all the answers I wanted, for that moment, it was enough.

Is it okay to be different from others? The truth is that it can be really tough. Standing out can suck, especially when it has to do with something everyone else has that you don't. In my case, it was the missing two fingers on my right hand, but for you, it might be the fact that you do not have a mother, or that you just lost a precious relationship, or maybe you do not understand things in the same way everybody else seems to grasp it.

However, it is okay to look in the mirror and accept that just as your face differs from everybody else, it is okay for your story to be different, too. You do not necessarily have to be happy about it, but thinking that way brings into perspective the fact that each person is working out their own story, and just because their challenge is not as visible as yours, it doesn't mean they aren't working through something too.

Growing Up

I grew up in a great community. It was a dream neighborhood for many parents, so I didn't know how harsh the world could be on people who were different until I had to go to elementary school.

Very few people were looking at my face on my first day at school. It seemed like my hand was the center of attention because my classmates stared continuously at it while asking me endless questions.

I hated the attention. I wasn't sure how to answer the questions, as the analogy my mom had told me did not seem to work with them. How could I explain that I had become aware I was alive, only to discover I was very different from everybody else? There was no explanation for that. It just simply was.

However, it was hard to get angry at the questions, especially as I grew older. People are fascinated by things they cannot explain or things that go beyond what they know - so it made sense for them to be curious. At the time, though, I did not appreciate it.

So, I started to hide. I would hide my hands in mittens and gloves or long-sleeved shirts during the winter until it got too hot to defend wearing them. And I would always have my right hand in my pocket. The truth is, I didn't want to explain myself to anyone. I wanted to be known as Jason - not the boy with three fingers.

It didn't mean I didn't have friends, though. In the apartment complex where I grew up, I had Riki, my comrade, in the water gun fights we had with a neighboring apartment complex. There was also Khalid, whom I assisted in devouring the white chocolates his grandma would bring from the factory where she worked, and

Taju, whom I grew up with because our moms went to the same school.

As I grew older, I also had friends like Jesse and Safar. They were snow shovel buddies, and we earned quite an amount every winter. I also had a friend group – Ian, Aaron, Rande'(R.I.P.), and I- and we bonded because of our love for wrestling. We would even have WWE Pay Per View viewing parties at each other's houses with an endless flow of pizza.

Having friends like this reminded me that I wasn't the odd one out every time. They had my back and were the kind of friends who would get into fights on my behalf. So, I had something to be grateful for, even while trying to figure out how to fit in at school. It didn't mean school was horrible, though, because the teachers knew to set excellence as a benchmark and would challenge us to be our best.

But, the insecurities I felt weren't so easy to let go of, and sometimes, I would ask my parents and myself repeatedly why it had to be me. I didn't want to be different and didn't care that everybody was unique in their own way, so why did I have to be born that way?

However, at this point in my life, when it was so easy to lean on the fact that I didn't have it as easy as others did, I am grateful for my parents. They didn't let me make any excuses, and they constantly reminded me that I could still do everything every other kid could do, even better than them. If I couldn't do something with my right hand, they would ask me to practice and practice again with my left hand. They would even tell my teachers not to take it easy on me and to treat me like everyone else. And they did all this while letting me know I was loved, valued, and not allowed to think less of myself.

To teach me that I could do whatever I wanted despite my handicap, my parents allowed me to explore as much as I wanted when it came to sports. I could play soccer, tennis, karate, basketball and baseball. The only sport I was never allowed to play was football, as I had a small stature, and my mom didn't want all the big guys in football making a sandwich with me.

These experiences built a confidence in me that serves me to this day. I learned practically that there was very little I couldn't do by doing the very things I would have thought my handicap would prevent me from doing. If my right hand couldn't manage it, my left hand was there to pick up the slack.

I became ambidextrous in the process. For tennis, my forehand swing was with my left hand, and I had a two-handed backhand swing. In baseball, I could catch with my right-handed baseball glove and throw with my left hand, even though my right hand was dominant. My mom took it a step further by personalizing a batter's glove for me so that it fit comfortably without the empty glove fingers hanging in the way.

Apart from improving my motor skills, sports helped me become more outgoing while allowing me to show the other kids that I could do everything they could, even with my three fingers. I am pretty sure it was their first time seeing someone with three fingers who could play like them, compete fairly, and even beat them - sometimes.

Thinking about it now, it's easy to see that the greatest advantage I gained from learning to do things others would assume I could not do was the fact that it upped my confidence levels - in those days, my confidence was through the roof after each achievement - and also set me up to try more complicated things later in life.

It also helped me teach others to give me a level playing field. It's common to see people try to be considerate because they see you have a challenge, so they do not offer you roles that they think would be too hard for you, or, without any bad intentions, they make decisions on your behalf that excludes you out of the very things you want.

While one of the things I thought I was doing was proving myself to my peers, I realize now that I was teaching them the right way to treat me. I was teaching them that it was okay to overlook my challenge and eradicate the wrongly placed good-intentioned consideration they had for me.

It is so easy to blame the people around you for not being able to understand that you are more than your challenges, but it is also vital to note that it is your responsibility to show them how you want to be treated.

Jason A. Jones

Finding Music

A large part of my life now is in the entertainment industry. But, my love for entertainment started even before I thought of making it a life-long career. My first encounter with music was with my father - even now, I can picture us listening to music and dancing in the living room. Although I couldn't describe it then, I realize now that music and dance always seemed to call out to something within me.

My grandmother had one of those shelf-sized stereos with a record and tape player that my older cousins and I would listen to and dance to.

I was always around music, from mixtapes to instruments to the microphone, and would even purchase blank tapes and record music off the radio and blend them. One day, I decided my self-made mixtapes needed something and got a microphone to infuse rap into the recordings.

One of the things I didn't like about elementary school - for all its advantages - was that I couldn't play the drums because our budget had run out, and there weren't any more drumsticks and pads to accommodate the new intakes. However, my love for music made me continue to pursue the available instruments, which turned out to be the trumpet, trombone, violin, and saxophone. I decided to pick the saxophone, and I think that was the first time my band teacher, Mr. Filipone, ever saw someone with three fingers attempt to play the saxophone.

The saxophone has twenty-three keys, with a very significant weight that the player has to bear with his body, but with a strap over my neck and shoulder, I was able to play it. However, it was heavy, especially when I had to walk a mile home from school, and after walking home with the saxophone in the rain several times, I decided to hand it in and switch to playing the trombone.

Compared to my determination to keep playing sports despite the initial difficulties, I now realize resilience doesn't always come in one form. Sometimes, it is also present when you realize something is not for you and are willing to try something else.

Middle School

I wonder if there will ever be a time when a fresh adventure doesn't come with equal bits of fear and excitement. Middle school was the adventure I had been anticipating, like a child looking forward to growing up, and it was exciting to think that I would be in a much larger school with kids from different elementary schools. Plus, the independence that came with it was overwhelming - I would have multiple teachers and not have to stay in one class all day. I was so excited.

As much as my excitement during this period makes me laugh, it's also made me realize how vital it is to allow ourselves to be happy and excited. Adulthood comes with a "done-it-all-seen-it-all" perspective that colors our experiences as meh. We expect nothing to last, so we forget to take joy in them since we already know a day will come when they might not be there anymore.

In retrospect, however, I'm learning from my eleven-year-old self. It is entirely okay to be excited about new things. We shouldn't be so cautious that we never let ourselves fly. Do not be so sure it will turn out badly that you're already sad on the first day. Constantly fight against being jaded. It's okay to bask in the euphoria of the moment.

I was also scared about starting middle school. What would I do when kids that I didn't know noticed my hand and asked me many questions or made jokes? Would I have to prove myself all over again?

I walked into school that first day with a false sense of bravado. My parents had already taught me to take things with my chin up, and my head held high, and I was going to do that even if there was a part of me that was afraid. However, it seemed I had been scared for nothing because I saw my first familiar face as I walked into the hall. I had never been so happy to hear a "Hey Tweet!" a nickname that I picked up at summer camp.

The first day set the pace for the rest of my middle school years. Having so many familiar faces prevented teasing to an extent, and I joined the soccer team, which meant I had a team that had my back. Soccer was a great experience since I played in elementary school, and I pretty much ruled the backfield as a defender. During that time, I met my first real girlfriend. I would walk her home every day, and she was my first real experience in being gentlemanly. My mother had taught me well.

A sad occurrence came during one of my home games when I collided with the opposing team's player and bruised my collarbone. I still remember the pain so vividly and how it felt like every bone in my body was being hit with a sledgehammer during every bump on my way to the hospital.

Thankfully, it wasn't as serious as it felt, and I was allowed to go home after getting a brace.

A few months later, I had gotten back to 100%, but I still had the brace on. I had also begun to nurture a desire to try my hand at basketball, so I tried out for the team. During summer, I attended summer camp at the Neighborhood House, and since I had become great at basketball, I made the first cut when I tried out.

However, we had to play Shirts vs Skins during tryouts for the second cut. My coach could see my collarbone brace since I was on the Skins team, and we had to play shirtless. He was worried about my injury, even though it had healed and I didn't make the final cut.

I didn't feel good about being cut, but I decided my next year at school, which was also the beginning of high school for me, the team would find me at basketball tryouts again.

High School

I love the way the movies paint high school. As confusing as it is, with teenagers and the insecurities that abound at that age, it also seems straightforward with the different cliques with unwritten entry rules. There are the jocks - the athletic cool guys who seem to get all the girls. There are the arty students - the creative, deep ones who might be cool or not, depending on the school.

The cheerleaders are the pretty girls who are the center of attention. There's the BFFs - the clique formed outside of high school with a bond no one even tries to break, and who don't care about what the people on the outside think. There are the geeks (or nerds) - no one ever thinks they're cool, even though everyone recognizes they've got the smarts and need their help occasionally.

In reality, things are not so clear-cut. Sometimes, there's a mixture, and an arty kid is also an athletic one, or sometimes, someone like me with three fingers makes the cut for the freshman basketball team.

I like to think that sometimes life equips you with survival skills for the future because we often find ourselves using the skills we honed over the years to get into the race or even make a name for ourselves. In my case, life had taught me I could do anything I put my mind to - if I wanted to, and people's expectations of me couldn't stop the fact that I could be anything I chose.

3 The Hard Way

So, were there surprised faces when I made the basketball team as a starting point guard? Of course. But that's the thing about expectations - they are never solid until you prove them wrong or right. And, boy, did I prove them wrong!

I still think my parents must have had some insight into my life when they had me focus on sports. And I am grateful for the things it helped me achieve. Apart from feeding my competitive spirit, it impacted my self-esteem greatly and made me realize the value of teams.

As much as we try to be independent as humans and find ourselves as individuals, there's great profit to being a part of a whole. And that is something we should never let ourselves ignore. Although I can only say these things from my vantage point in the present, looking back at my past, I realize that one of the biggest secrets to overcoming life's obstacles is having a solid support system.

From my parents to my brother to my friends and teammates, I see how having these people at my back helped shape me into the man I am now.

I didn't get to stay in the basketball team for very long as a new kid with a killer crossover took my spot as the starting point guard, but even though I had to sit on the bench, I still got to travel with the team and enjoy the camaraderie and fun. I moved on to soccer and tennis. For soccer, I started on the JV Soccer team and immediately got higher up due to my defense skills. I won a round-robin on the tennis team and started on the varsity team playing doubles along with my friend John and Cameron.

Apart from sports, I joined clubs that caught my interest during my sophomore year. There was the gentlemen's club, the robotics team, Upward Bound - a pre-college summer program for high school students- and the Sigma Beta Club, part of a fraternity that assisted young men in getting ready for college. These clubs helped me work on my shyness by forcing me to be out there, prepared me for college way ahead of time, and showed me true brotherhood.

During my junior year, I picked up two jobs. The first was cutting the grass and cleaning the trash for the perimeter of my housing development, and the second was at McDonald's, where I went from being a cashier to cooking to running the drive-thru window.

While working at McDonald's, a particular incident stood out for me because of its impact on my brother and what taught me about resilience and being an example to another person.

My first car - a prized possession - had a faulty transmission, and though my mother wanted to get rid of the car, I didn't want to let it go. However, I didn't have enough money for a replacement, so I decided to work more hours to raise the money.

To do this, I had to put in countless hours. My life at the time was basically from the house in the early mornings to work and then home in the late evenings. I was working 2 to 3 shifts to raise the money and had to decline all offers from my friends to go to parties or events. I would even ride my bike or walk to work and hitch a ride with my mom when it was dark or the weather was inclement. I remember during the winters, Safar, Saleem, Jesse, Ronnell and I would walk house to house shoveling sidewalks and porches to make extra money.

Most people couldn't believe I would sacrifice this much time, fun, and my whole summer to get my car fixed, but I had a culture now of not letting anything stop me from achieving what was possible, and I didn't mind sacrificing to get it done. I had my eye fixed on my goal.

I eventually did get enough money saved up for my transmission, but that was not even the highlight of having achieved my goal. Instead, it was getting a greeting card from my brother to celebrate my accomplishment.

The greeting card, simple as it was, meant a lot to me. It told me he had seen me put in the work and respected my drive and determination to achieve what I had set my sights on. It meant so much to me because having my younger brother recognize what sacrifice was, and its importance was a big deal. It also told me I had taught him something that would stay with him for a long time. And that was a huge privilege.

It later turned out that my work culture had been so impressive that the manager asked if I would like to train to be a manager. It was a pat on the back, but I declined because college was what I wanted to do next.

Chapter 3
Center Stage

Adulthood can be scary. That's why college is one of the most important aspects of life for the average young adult. They realize it might be their last chance before responsibility comes in its full glory, and they know it is a ticking clock to the end of the times when they could do certain things and get away with it.

Of course, it isn't the same for everyone, but even though I had my share of growing up while I was younger, I still felt a sense of responsibility.

I didn't have the best SAT score, but I made up for it with community service activities and intense participation in sports. That meant I got two partial out-of-state scholarships, one to play tennis and the other to play soccer. Unfortunately, neither was enough to cover the whole year's tuition, so I decided to attend a university in my home state—William Paterson University in New Jersey.

My college being so close to home helped make adjusting to a completely different experience easier. I was just an hour from home, and although I didn't intend to use that card often, knowing I had a safe space so close to me was comforting.

I was also a bit nervous because I was worried about meeting completely new people who would be curious about my three fingers. I had also always nursed a secret fear about girls not wanting to be with me because of my condition - I always worried they would think my condition was hereditary and they wouldn't like someone long-term who might pass this on to their kids.

I shouldn't have worried so much, though. It turns out that there are genuine humans out there who just like you for you. Added to that, on my first day on campus, I met a lot of familiar faces. They were faces I recognized from my graduating class and those who graduated a year or two before me.

One day, I wore my Sigma Beta shirt, which opened the door to meeting other people in the same sorority and fraternity ties. Most of the connections I had made in high school through the various clubs I was a part of were working for me in the present, too.

I was studying Communications with a concentration in TV/Radio Production. My love for music, dance, and everything to do with entertainment was still alive, and I had a goal of transitioning fully into the entertainment space after college.

In the second semester of my first year in college, I decided to pledge to Phi Beta Sigma Fraternity, Inc. and became one of the youngest members in the state. This decision expanded my network greatly, as I met fraternity members from other colleges and universities and made new friends around the East Coast.

In my sophomore year, I got jobs on campus as a student technology consultant and worked the cash register at Best Buy off campus. My grades were good; I had a car and was pretty comfortable. I also became a part of my college's step team as I had previous experience stepping, and I got to travel across the Tri-state for competitions with other step teams members from different colleges.

During junior year, I started looking for internships and landed my first through a college career counselor at Automatic Productions - a subsidiary of Sony Music Entertainment.

I loved that job. It was the freshness of the experience, coupled with the fact that it looked like my life was opening up in the direction of the path I had always dreamt of. I was also learning many new things and making vital industry network connections. The job involved assisting in organizing music tape catalog information, running errands from the studio to the corporate office, and setting up and breaking down video shoots. And twice every week, I jumped on a bus to New York to learn, work, and learn even more.

Right before my internship ended, management offered me a position as a production assistant. My job description was to help with video shoots, and I did this until I was let go after two weeks due to budgetary constraints due to the Sony/BMG mergers.

Being let go made me sad and upset. Even though I was still confident that another opportunity would come, I felt I still had so much to learn at the job. However, there was nothing I could do about it but be grateful I learned as much as I did. It was a priceless experience that I knew would be useful in the future.

Senior year came, and it seemed like a journey that looked like it would last forever, went by too fast. I wanted to build my career immediately after graduation, so I focused on that. It was scary, though. My class was graduating 3,000 students, and that was just in my school. The competition was fierce, and I knew it might take a lot of work to land a TV or Radio Job.

I started asking around and telling the people in my network about my interest in finding a job. A fraternity brother helped me get a job at one of the hottest radio stations in NYC - Hot 97. I started work in the promotions department, where my role was to help promote the station and set up DJs for different events in the city.

I had a lot of fun working at this job because I was in the entertainment industry - my eternal love - and I got to meet a lot of talent and attend music events. The only drawback was the fact that it was a part-time job. Fortunately, I picked up another part-time job promoting Cadillac vehicles at all the home New York Jets games on the weekends.

I still needed a job that brought in a more stable income since I had graduated from school at the time. So, I applied to temp agencies. It wasn't easy getting a job because companies in NYC seemed to prefer candidates in the city, and even though I lived 25-30 miles away by car with the option of commuting by bus or train, I seemed to get disqualified after each interview. It was also possible that I wasn't as qualified as others.

The temp agency finally found a job for me at LabCorp, where I put together clinical trial kits for doctors and shipped them out. It was a straightforward task, and the money was good for a guy just out of college. Even though I wasn't building my dream career yet, the part-time jobs still helped me keep my toe in the entertainment waters.

I still looked forward to a full career in entertainment, but I didn't realize that life was about to place my entire journey on pause.

PART 2

FACING CHALLENGES

Chapter 4
The Accident

Half the time, life presents itself as the big bad guy trying to fight against us. Things happen without explanation, and it is often tempting to close our eyes and give up.

Fighting our way through things can be challenging, and I appreciate you - the reader - for having the grit to decide you will try again. The act of seeking hope and a reason to keep on is beautiful and something to be proud of.

I never had any reason to think I would have a life-halting accident - we never really do. I was just the typical guy with a job, side gigs, and a dream to delve into the career I really wanted in the near future. And I had been on that track for two years. Life was boring and uneventful, and while I sometimes had an itch for more, I didn't completely hate where I was.

The day it happened was uneventful, too. It was Wednesday, November 21, 2007, a day before Thanksgiving. I woke up feeling the same, got ready for work using the same routine, started the car, and picked up my colleague. I often go through that morning's events in my head to see if anything felt different. Did dropping my car keys that morning signal something ominous?

The accident happened while we were driving to work. I was two blocks from my house when an SUV smashed into the driver's side, forcing my car to spin and hit a tree and brick wall in front of a house. I don't remember much else - these things tend to happen like they're happening to someone else because your brain cannot quite comprehend that it is happening for real, at least until the pain hits.

I still do not remember if I screamed. I only remember fighting to gain control of the steering wheel through the sound of a ringing in my ears and feeling like my heart had stopped. I remember thinking about my mom and brother and everything I hadn't done yet. And then I remember feeling blank, like I was in a void.

Someone must have dialed 911 because the firefighters were cutting my car door off and trying to pull me out of the car. When they asked if I was okay, I nodded blankly. I had lost my glasses and was trying to get my bearings even though it was proving to be a futile attempt. They asked me if I had a passenger, and completely forgetting about my colleague, I shook my head no. I was so out of it that when they asked if I was sure, I named someone I had driven with a week ago.

My responses must have told them I was way out of it because the next thing I knew, they were bundling me onto the stretcher and escorting me to the ambulance. Before I left, they told me there had been someone else in the car with me, and I asked if they were okay. My colleague was okay but had a knee injury, and while I was relieved it wasn't more severe, I was still so confused that I couldn't focus on what they said after that.

In the ambulance, I gained some of my bearings and called my mom to let her know I was on the way to the hospital. She had seen the ambulance on her way to work and made a detour when she saw the emergency lights and traffic ahead of her.

I still get jitters when I think about the hospital - not because I had to stay for very long, but because it seemed to signify the proverbial stamp on losing the majority of all I had worked for. I was diagnosed with short-term memory loss, neck and back injuries, and a torn rotator cuff, and I had to get eleven stitches to close the gash on my eyelid.

It is weird how when things out of our control happen to us, we feel pitiful - almost like it is our fault somehow. We have all this pain stored up inside, and since there's nobody to blame, we blame ourselves. We begin to think of all the ways it must have been our fault and what we could have done to avoid it.

That was what happened to me. Even though a corner of my heart recognized the blessing in being able to walk out of the hospital in one piece, especially when the driver of a huge Toyota Sequoia had hit my comparably tiny two-door Honda Civic in a bid to beat the red light, I still couldn't seem to bring myself out of my gloom. A part of me knew enough to be thankful I had survived, but the other part of me just kept wondering why this had happened to me.

Thanksgiving the next day was a horrible day for me. I had no appetite and was highly medicated. The only thing I could focus on was the pain. I just wanted it to hurt less, and not even my brother and mother trying to cheer me up and ask what I needed made it better.

It would take eight months before I recovered fully. I wasn't able to move my arm six inches from my waist for some time, and I had to sleep on my back because the stitches in my eyelid meant my left eye was completely shut for a few weeks. From weekly doctor appointments to the chiropractor to ease the pain in my neck and back and regain movement in my arm to therapy, my life was both busy and an emotional and physical rollercoaster.

My therapy sessions were with an emotional and cognitive therapist so I could learn how to cope with my injuries and relearn how to retain information. The accident had affected my frontal lobe, which meant I was having trouble retaining short-term memories. Therapy helped me learn how to stack and retain information and kept me from giving up from the frustration of repeatedly trying the same thing.

For someone who had learned never to give up early in life and to always find a way because our goals were possible if we kept at them, I had to learn a deeper chapter of that lesson. The question being put in front of me now was, "What if it takes longer?" "What if you have to wait while feeling like your whole life is passing you by and still see no results despite all the efforts you're putting in?" "What if trying again and again wasn't good enough?"

In the past, it was easy for me to calculate a response time. I was a sports guy, and I knew there was a high probability of scoring if I calculated my moves correctly. I knew I could get my car back in working order if I calculated my pay and dedicated the corresponding hours to get the needed amount. I knew that if I practiced long enough, I would get better at any sport. I knew to keep going because I could tell what would happen at the end.

But this time, I didn't know. I didn't know if I would ever get full movement in my arms. I didn't know if I would ever get my memory back in full working order. I didn't know if I could get my life back on track. I didn't know how (or even what) to calculate this time, especially since all the effort I put in felt like a joke, and I felt so out of control.

I was tired. I was angry. And, I was afraid. I still don't know how I managed to keep going. But, somehow, I did. I had a group therapy session as part of my healing process, and that helped me put a lot of things in perspective. It made me understand that no matter how bad my situation was, someone had it worse, and I wasn't the only one going through hard stuff.

That didn't make me feel better, as there's no joy in comparing your suffering to another's and then using theirs as a meter for whether you should be grateful or not. But it did make me feel seen and heard and like I still belonged somewhere, no matter what. It also made me learn to give it time. Even though I couldn't predict how long it would take, sharing with them made me realize that putting in my best while giving it time was the best I could do for myself. Besides, if I gave up, I would lose the thread of hope I was desperately clinging to.

Even though I was trying my best to get back to normal, it didn't mean the whole world paused to wait for me to get better. I had to visit different insurance doctors from the insurance companies to verify my injuries so I could get some of my bills paid. I also had to forget about driving in the meantime and rely on someone else to help me move around. Even the basic things like cutting grass or attending social functions with friends that had come so easily to me weren't a part of my life anymore.

I had lost all my jobs, but thankfully, I was still living at home with my mom and didn't have a lot of bills to take care of. I would also get several visitors coming to check up on me, and although I hadn't wanted anyone to see me in my beat-up state, I learned to be grateful that I had all these people who cared deeply for me.

The biggest lesson I learned during this time was that it was okay to feel like giving up as long as I never gave up. Life happens to each of us in phases; sometimes, we do not even have the strength to face the next day. And it's okay to feel that way. It's okay to admit that we have nothing left to give. But, at the end of that admission, we must find that thin thread of hope and try again.

Taking a break is okay, but we must find it within ourselves to keep going.

Chapter 5
One Step Forward, Two Steps Back

It was eight months after my accident, and I felt ready to get back to work. Unfortunately, that meant I had to start job hunting since I had lost all my jobs after the accident because I wasn't a full-time employee.

Eight months was a long time in the job scenery, which became a disadvantage in my search for a job. Nobody wanted to hire someone with a huge gap in his resume, and the fact that I didn't live in New York City didn't help matters. I had to deal with rejection after rejection, and it was so much that I sometimes wondered why I had put in all that effort to get better, only to realize that the world had moved on without me and had no space for me anymore.

It felt like taking one step forward, only to be drawn two steps backwards by the obstacles in front of you. I'd usually wonder what I had done to deserve this and if this was how my life would turn out. Every dream I had now felt almost impossible, and it seemed like I was begging for even one ray of light.

It was hard then to see and be grateful for the things I still had. Even though I still had my mother, my most supportive pillar, and my brother, who would cheer me on and remind me of my past victories, all I could think of was how dark everything seemed. My unemployment and disability funds had run out, I was still paying my student loans, and I was racking up credit card expenses with no way to pay more than the minimum fees. The frustration and despair made it seem like the whole world was against me, and I began to allow my old fears to creep back in.

I would remember how people did not expect someone with three fingers to be able to do some of the things I did, and that led to me being afraid of not amounting to much and being scared of my future. I temporarily forgot how I had been able to surmount those fears and do the things I wanted to do by persevering because all I could think at that time were dark thoughts.

It didn't seem fair that my breakthrough moment was taking too long to come. It had started to feel like I was holding on to pipe dreams if I expected more from life than what seemed to be my portion.

Everything I was going through, even though false assumptions and fears were driving them, was very valid. The assumptions were false because there is no one portion allotted to you in life. Instead, you take as much out of life as you're willing to work towards. However, when everything seems dark, this assumption can seem so true that you become tempted to accept only crumbs.

It is also valid because these feelings are real, whether true or not, and it is vital to acknowledge them while working so as not to let them have power over you. When we go through the most challenging periods of our lives, we often forget all the good times and fail to recognize the good things and people around us.

One of the hacks to overcoming obstacles during hard times is to listen. There will be a lot of voices in your head and from the outside, and it is essential to be able to choose the voices to listen to during this time. Listen to the voice that tells you there's more to come, and it isn't over yet. While it might not look like it, that is the truth. Listen to the voice that tries to remind you how strong you are and how you overcame hard things in the past. Listen to the voice that tells you you're worth fighting for. And, listen to me - one who has gone through the hard stuff too - and can tell you it gets better.

It is going to be hard to listen to these good voices. They will either be too quiet amid all that's going on in your mind, or whatever they say will seem like a lie because everything you can see at the time tells you a different story.

On the other hand, it will be easy to listen to and accept the voices of doom and defeat. That is because they reinforce what you already feel. When they tell you you are nothing, it is easy to agree because, at that moment, you feel like nothing. When they tell you nobody loves you or is rooting for you, it is easy to accept that because you have perhaps experienced betrayal from people around you. But these things are not true, and it takes us being willing to look beyond what is happening at the moment and listening to the voices that tell us there is still more to come to be able to overcome the weight of dark times.

This was what I did to get the strength to continue trying in the face of all the rejections. I listened to the voice within me that told me I had overcome much worse, and instead of beating myself up for something that was not my fault, it was better to intensify my efforts.

I started to send out my resumé to every contact I had and some temp agencies. I didn't want to give up or accept no as an answer; eventually, it began to pay off.

Chapter 6
Odd Jobs, Big Dreams

The first job I got was from a temp agency. It was a two-month job, and my tasks were to put certified mail stickers on loan mailings. Every day, from 8 AM -2 PM, I had a mail bin full of envelopes to add the stickers to. Once I completed the bin, a fresh bin was waiting for me.

Even though I had hoped earnestly for a job, I would sometimes have depressing thoughts, wondering if this was what I had gotten a degree for. It was hard to reconcile the big dreams I had with what I was doing in the present at the time. However, I began to realize that the job was a blessing in disguise, as it helped me realize that even though I believed I was ready to go back into full-time work, the opposite was the case.

I would get exhausted before 2 PM from putting on the stickers, and I realized that I needed to slowly work my way back to working for long hours. And this job was the stepping stone I needed to recover fully.

After two months, the job ended, and I got another local temp job at a medical support manufacturer. This job differed from my last one, as it required me to be aware and attentive. My task was to work with a team of at least five people on a machine that turned every thirty seconds. Each station on the machine had a task for the final product to be fully functional and complete, as the whole system would stop if one position was slow or done wrong.

It was not an easy job because we had a target number each day, and failure to meet up would mean choosing between moving to another job or possible termination. I found that it helped me work on paying attention to detail, which I had been worried about because of the part of my head affected in the accident.

I was at this job for three months before I got another opportunity from another temp agency. My new job was at a motorcycle insurance company, where I scanned all claim info and submitted incoming payment information into the computer system.

At this job, I swung back into my usual grind of full-time hours and tested my ability to pay attention to detail. I was finally back to 100%. I continued working at this job for one year until I got an unexpected message.

An old co-worker I had worked with in college sent a message asking if I was still working at the radio station. I replied that I wasn't, and she asked if I was interested in a position back in the radio industry. I said yes and rapidly sent in my resumé.

It is often weird how, one day, you're going through the motions of life, and in the blink of an eye, an opportunity comes that changes your entire course and sets you on the path that leads to what you had always dreamed of. In retrospect, this must be what the people who advise you to hold on are talking about. They're perhaps talking about the doors that open unexpectedly while you are engrossed in doing all you can with what you have.

Within a week, I had an interview and was back in the entertainment industry. My new job threw me into a different aspect of the entertainment industry than I had been used to. I had previously worked at a hip hop and R&B station, but this new position was for a dance/pop/rock station, and it introduced me to new scenes in entertainment that gave me a fresh perspective into the industry that I am forever grateful for.

It turned out that my supervisor was the former President of the Greek Council I was a member of in college, and he remembered me from the monthly meetings and events I had attended. I hadn't realized that my early days of networking and being a part of social clubs would reap these kinds of fruits later in life, and it made me realize how important it was to be someone of great value wherever you are.

No matter your natural temperament, it is vital to forge connections through an exchange of value because these seeds later show up as trees to help keep you steady in the future.

3 The Hard Way

Although rewarding and emotionally satisfying, my radio job was a part-time job. Sometimes, I didn't have many hours, and I had a lot of free time where I wasn't doing much. So, I started a search for a full-time job. I applied to several and did some networking with my friends and family to see if they knew anyone in the industry.

To my surprise, I discovered that my aunt worked in the industry and had some connections at the jobs I had already applied for. Shortly after, I was invited for an interview for a new television production. At the interview, although they were curious about the gap in my resumé, they must have seen my drive and determination in how I had bounced back and had my foot in the entertainment industry.

I got a call for a second interview and went dressed to impress in a suit and tie. Imagine my surprise when one of the first questions the interviewer asked was why I was overdressed - apparently, the television world required just jeans and a t-shirt - and the executive in charge let me know that was what she wanted to see me in when I resumed work. In other words, I had gotten the job as a Production Assistant!

I threw myself into my job with all the enthusiasm I could muster. I finally got my chance in the entertainment industry and didn't want to mess up the opportunity. I had two jobs at radio and television, and for the next seven months, I worked both jobs.

While I knew it would be stressful, it seemed like a waste to let go of working in radio. The exposure and learning experiences it afforded me were too good to let go of, and I did think I could manage both quite well. My routine was to take a bus into New York City and then catch the train to New Jersey for my other job. Alternatively, I sometimes decided to drive to New Jersey, park my car, and take the train to New York before returning to New Jersey.

Sometimes, I slept in the conference room of the NYC job after a gig, so I would wake early in the morning, shower at the office before anyone came in, and be at my desk on time. In my overwhelming desire to do my best, I forgot I was human until my body began to create incidents to remind me.

I was running to deliver a tape to a studio one morning when I forgot where I was going in the middle of my trip. I stood, disoriented, at a corner in the middle of New York City and didn't know where I was going or even how to get back to my office. I started to panic when I tried to reach a co-worker, only to find that my cell had no service.

I was beginning to feel stirrings of fear in the pit of my stomach when I remembered that we had been taught during counseling to learn to stop everything and be patient when we felt panic attempting to overwhelm us. So, I tried to calm down, took a few deep breaths, and waited. I didn't mind the stares I was getting at the time, but later, I would remember the looks and realize that I needed to take responsibility for my well-being. It was no use burning out trying to do my best because if something happened to me, people would only look in pity, but they wouldn't be able to do anything for me. I was responsible for myself.

The counseling trick worked, and I was able to remember where I needed to go, but after that day, I quit my job at the radio station.

Two extremes can happen when we finally get something we had almost believed would never be possible. We either try to overcompensate by continuously trying to prove we are worthy of what we now have, or we self-sabotage. When we self-sabotage, we feel so unworthy of what we have that we unconsciously mess it up without being aware that whatever we're doing is a direct attempt to mess up an opportunity we're somehow so sure we will mess up eventually.

In my case, without knowing it, I was trying to overcompensate by grabbing the opportunities too tightly and being afraid of letting any of them go - even when it affected my health. A huge part of making it happen is accepting that it is yours, you deserve it, and while you're not going to mishandle the opportunity, you won't be a slave to it either.

After I resigned, I was more relaxed, which meant I could focus on my tasks more and volunteer for weekend production projects in the field. While I looked at these field projects as a fun and learning opportunity, the executive producers and crew saw it as dedication and an impressive demonstration of willpower, and my name began to make rounds in the department in a positive light.

In thirteen months, I received a promotion offer from management to become a coordinator in either the field department as a field department coordinator or in the post-production department as a music coordinator. I picked the music coordinator position since I had extensive experience in music.

Despite all my experience, however, I still had much to learn. One of my responsibilities was to expedite the delivery of music cue sheets to the Performance Rights Organization to ensure the writers and composers of the music we used got paid. I also pulled music for editors, live walkouts, and promotional usage.

My job got even more exciting because I had many opportunities to network with other entertainment professionals and panels in NYC after we taped shows. I also took a music supervision class at NYU during the summer, and I was looking forward to becoming the best in my field. At least until circumstances pulled the carpet from under me. Again.

PART 3

EMBRACING THE JOURNEY

Chapter 7
Something Unexpected

If there's anything my journey through life has taught me, it would be that things happen unexpectedly. This applies to the good and positive experiences and the bad and negative stuff.

The best we can do is to prepare ourselves by getting our minds to understand that no matter what comes, there's always a way to overcome it, and when good things happen, we need to maximize it.

It was certainly unexpected to discover I would lose a job I had put my best into for six years. Somehow, we have been taught to expect that when we put our best efforts into something, it should last forever - just like a car continues to run as long as you fuel it. However, things sometimes turn out differently. Sometimes, the vehicle develops faults simply fueling it cannot fix, or in other cases, it is just time to let that car go. And this isn't about cars.

In the entertainment industry, most productions take a hiatus at the end of May, go for a break during summer, and return in August before the new season premieres in September. At the end of the season, just before our break, we usually have a wrap party and exit meetings. The exit meeting was a management review, where the management would review your performance that year, and you got to find out if you were still a part of the staff in the coming year.

However, it was odd this time, as I had yet to be called in for a meeting. I tried to request a meeting several times but was stonewalled and given no response. Assuming an error, I went in person to request a meeting and finally had one on the calendar.

The meeting went well; I had a good track record and received a sterling report. The management told me there was no start date yet for my renewal, but I would receive a call sometime in August. Satisfied with that, I planned a few trips for my break.

During mid-August, I called and left a voicemail message with my supervisor. However, I still hadn't received a callback at the end of August, so I decided to call again. Again, there was no response. The following Monday, I went to the office and found that there had been several changes I was unaware of.

The population at the office had dwindled, and my heart skipped a beat when I noticed several familiar faces weren't at their desks. I went to my desk to start the day off, and alarm bells went off in my head when my password didn't work, even after several attempts. I made a complaint to the IT department, and they gave me access, but the alarm bells in my head were ringing even louder, and I began to retrieve a few of my things from my desk.

The next thing I knew, an assistant told me the executives were in a meeting, and I was to wait for them. After an hour, a new manager told me to go to our branch across town for a meeting. The alarms in my head were almost deafening at this point as it was obvious something was wrong.

I made my way across town and was told that there were budget cuts and that the company would be unable to renew my contract. I received a severance package, got a good pat on the back, had my badge retrieved, and was sent home with no prospect of new opportunities at the company.

I still can't remember how I got to the Port Authority Bus Station that day. The only thing I remember was feeling like the walk would never end - almost like there was no end in sight, and I would have to walk down the road forever.

I eventually got on a bus, and I remember avoiding the other passengers and sitting in the first corner I could find because all I wanted was to be left alone. Unfortunately, my phone started ringing just as I took my seat, and it turned out to be my supervisor.

He kept calling me back to back, and I remember wondering to myself if time had stopped for him and had only just started because I couldn't understand why he would leave me hanging, only to have somebody else drop the bomb and then start calling me to warn me of it. I let the call go to voicemail and didn't bother to return it.

My mind was a warzone of "If only", and I couldn't stop wondering why I hadn't received the courtesy of being told beforehand. A few months before we went on hiatus, I received an offer for a position at another organization, but I declined, thinking my future at my current company was set. Now, I was out of a job, and I had spent a whole summer I could have used to search for jobs on trips, and all positions were now taken since it was already September.

After being let go, I was bitter for a while, but I had learned that it was every man for himself in the entertainment business - probably in all kinds of business, too. No matter where we find ourselves, we must always care for ourselves first.

While it doesn't stop us from putting our best into a job, ensuring your contract looks out for you instead of covering only areas related to your loyalty to the company is essential. Ensure your contract has an agreed amount of time for notice, have your company agree to write you an honest report of your activities on the job, as this can serve as a recommendation letter, and always look out for ways to develop yourself even while on the job.

That said, it is also vital to understand that unexpected things like this might still happen even when you take the best precautions, so ensure you develop a mindset that enables you to bounce back from anything and everything that comes your way.

On getting home that day, I immediately contacted a lawyer to review my severance package and applied for unemployment. I also started reaching out to my network and applying for jobs everywhere within the industry. However, considering the hiring season had just ended, I got negative responses everywhere I turned.

Thinking back on those times, I can see that my response to setbacks during this time was different. I could still think on my feet, and even though I was angry and hurt, I could still pick the lessons and start thinking of what to do next. That showed that I had learned something from my past setbacks and had become a stronger person through those ordeals.

While negative experiences are never something we pray for or expect, we can turn them into positive experiences when we are able to gain lessons and look past the scars. That's not to say that the scars disappear, only that it is possible to live beyond them and become stronger because of them.

Two weeks after losing my job, I decided to stop complaining, thinking of what could have been "if only" and taking matters into my own hands. I began to analyze the situation to see what I could do next by asking myself questions like, "What did I like at my previous job?" "What could I do to have more stability at my next job?"

Since one of my tasks at my previous job was keeping track of artist agreements so I could answer any questions about a song within an agreement, I wanted to learn more about agreements. There and then, I decided to look into becoming a paralegal.

Chapter 8
A New Act

There were certainly people who thought my decision to move suddenly into a completely new field was weird and worrisome. I had questions and statements like, "Are you sure?" "You shouldn't worry yourself so much; a job in your industry will surely come." "Are you sure you aren't giving up?"

In all truth, I had also asked myself those questions. I was still very interested in the entertainment industry, and it did seem weird to move to an entirely different field suddenly. However, as different a field as being a paralegal seemed, it still had a considerable connection to the entertainment industry. One poorly written contract or a mistake in a contract that isn't discovered in time can spell doom for the artist or entertainment company.

So, while it seemed different, it was related, and I found it exciting and adventurous to do the next best thing while I waited for what I considered best to become mine. In a way, it was also extra preparation for a time when I would have that which I had always wanted.

I started researching accredited local and online New Jersey schools, and Fairleigh Dickinson University caught my eye. I attended their open house for the program, and while I was there, I knew that this was where I needed to be. They offered tuition discounts if you had a lawyer recommend you, so I immediately drafted a letter and hand-delivered it to my attorney's office.

A week later, the lawyer sent in a response requesting that we meet. We met, and after discussing my plan, I had a letter ready and got the discount on my tuition. For the next eight months, I threw myself wholeheartedly into my course. I was taking morning and evening classes, and I can tell you they rate really high on the list of all the hard things I've done in my lifetime.

I liked some of the courses I was offering, like Business Law, Real Estate Law, and Intellectual Property Law, because they were very practical and familiar. However, other courses, like Family Law, Elder Law, and Legal Writing, were more challenging. Still, I applied my mind to learning them because it was an exciting experience to learn new things and make strides in areas I couldn't have imagined.

In my last semester, I began looking for jobs. The school's career counselor assisted in helping us locate potential paralegal jobs, and I went on several interviews in the entertainment and legal industry. At the interviews, I was often asked about my career shift because of the swerve I had made. I continually had to explain the reasons for my present career trajectory and my plans moving forward.

I graduated and obtained my paralegal certificate after eight months, and although I couldn't secure a job, the entire experience changed the way I think forever. I now put extra thought into everyday things because I know several laws are attached to them, and I have learned to be a better calculated risk taker instead of an all-in risk taker.

After graduating, I kept searching for a position online, and one day, I got a hit from the school's career website. It was a job in the legal industry, and I got an invite to an interview one week after I applied. Unfortunately, although I had nailed the interview, they responded a day later that somebody else had gotten the position.

Trying to remain positive, I thanked the supervisor for calling me back to let me know and asked that he do me the favor of keeping my resumé on file in case any other new opportunities arose. I'm glad I thought to ask for that because a month later, there was an opening, and I went in for another interview. A week later, I had my first job as a paralegal.

The contract was to last for three to four months; however, I must have impressed them very much with my can-do attitude and strong work ethic because the position turned into a full-time role in which I would eventually spend four years.

My duties at the beginning of the role were to research statutes and cases to ensure their accuracy and create hyperlinks with them for an e-formatted book. However, the role provided me with a very vast learning experience because, at the end of it, I had learned to use Pitney Bowes copying and mailing machines, plan events, and set up/break down legal seminars across the state and had numerous opportunities to network with judges and lawyers.

I was learning to adjust to different people and environments, and I am grateful for that experience. I was still interested in the entertainment space, and I kept my eyes and ears open in case I could pick up an opportunity. I would even frequently use my spare time to attend entertainment panels, and I also took up a part-time job with Uber to make some additional income.

My stories as an Uber Driver could fill up another book as I met people from all walks of life and witnessed several fascinating perspectives. Discovering the many different viewpoints from other cultures, family traditions, and societal influences was exhilarating. And I sometimes felt like I was experiencing different parts of the world.

Although there were sometimes passengers that made me wonder why I had ever accepted their ride requests, I would usually bump into passengers I could learn something from. I had learned the importance of engaging in exciting conversations, and I often started one with my passengers. I would learn about their career paths, education, mindset, and other life lessons that helped me immensely.

I would also return the favor by telling them bits and pieces about myself and answering their questions about my hand whenever any of them was bold enough to ask. At this time, my three fingers had become a part of me, and I no longer needed to hide or explain it to others. It just felt normal, like a hand would feel. So, I never minded when I got asked questions about it. Although, most people were too shy to ask on most days.

Something else that meeting different people and hearing their stories taught me was that each of us has our own struggles, and each person has what another person wishes for, no matter how disadvantaged they might feel. I was learning to take nothing for granted and always to be grateful for everything I had.

I also began to take my health more seriously and started a routine of working out and mindful eating. I would prepare my lunch at home to control my eating habits and save some money, and during my lunch breaks, I would eat and then go for a thirty-minute walk. I did this every day without fail, except on the days it rained when I would sit back in to read a self-help book. I discovered that reading them helped me enforce a positive mindset and gave me a broader outlook on life's tendencies.

I also began to attend a spin class to help step up my workouts and put myself in a beneficial environment where I could replenish my social batteries. I had learned that work was not everything and that it was crucial to create a life outside of work where you explore your passions and do things that put a little step in your work.

My Uber rides also taught me that conversations are vital to the human psyche. One-time discussions with people you were sure would never see again had a unique calming effect because you could talk without fear of judgment. But, I found that building relationships with people you could talk to and be yourself around was even more rewarding. I had begun to place a heavy emphasis on not just networking but also consciously building relationships where you can relax and be without any pressure for performance.

I spent four years exploring life outside the one I had always dreamed of in the entertainment industry. Although I would eventually take steps to get back into the world of entertainment, I am very grateful for the time I spent trying new things. It is something I would recommend for anyone because new life experiences and being in places where you never thought you would stand have a way of bringing out new and wonderful things in you.

Also, it's never too late to learn something completely new and out of your usual zone, so why not give it a try?

Chapter 9
Recasting My Role

Have you ever wondered when it's okay to give up? If you've tried and tried again, shouldn't you give up even if it's something that keeps ringing in your heart and resonating in your soul?

There's no straightforward answer to this. For some, it is best to move on to other things while accepting that what they have seen in their mind might never come. For others, it is best to keep trying and waiting for life to bring an opportunity that validates all they have prepared for.

The truth is, neither choice is easy. For me, I chose to learn something completely new and put myself entirely into it so I could enjoy it while still holding on to my dreams and looking out for opportunities. In retrospect, I can say this is one of the best ways to go about it.

Do not let yourself enter a limbo state because your dream isn't materializing yet. It is okay to try something completely new and have other dreams. If your initial dream still weighs heavy on your heart, ensuring you're preparing for it while exploring a different thing is still possible. And it's okay to come back to it too. After all, if the dream won't let you go, it's your responsibility to make it happen.

I excelled as a paralegal, exceeding expectations, and was trusted with more responsibilities as time passed. However, I still yearned to be in the entertainment industry, so I started looking for jobs again.

I would apply, get several callbacks, have interviews, and get many questions on why a paralegal would be interested in the entertainment industry - especially since I was still in the legal sector and had to explain while connecting the dots to how my past and current duties made me perfect for the position.

Although they understood, it would be a series of rinsing and repeating the same actions for the next six months with no luck. At the time, I wondered why I was so interested in a job in the entertainment industry, especially since I had what most people would consider a steady job, even with its drawbacks.

However, several years later, I can see that it was like something was calling out my name, and I had to answer no matter what. Even if I tried and failed a thousand times, I had to try again because that was where I wanted to be, and settling for what was available didn't make sense.

I believe that distinguishes a dream you should keep fighting for from a dream you should let go of. Does it keep calling your name? If yes, then keep pursuing it. Are you letting go of your dreams because they seem too hard to achieve? If that's the only reason, it is vital you cultivate the discipline to keep trying. Are you letting go of your dreams only because people think it's best to let it go? If that's the only reason, please don't let it go.

I have discovered that one of the truest joys in life is being true to yourself. Chase after that thing that seems impossible by learning the best ways to get there and preparing for it.

There will be times when you have to say goodbye to things you have always wanted, and the best way to tell is that you will know, no matter how much you try to deny it. Instead of excuses like, "It's too hard," you will need no excuse when it's time to let go - you'll recognize it's time, as long as you're ready, to be honest with yourself.

It can be hard to admit this, but one sign you should look out for is that you're letting your life pause because of this dream. Something worth pursuing does not drain the life out of you. Instead, it has the ability to infuse life into you.

It is time to reassess if it drains the life out of you, making you feel frustrated and hopeless. It is also time to reassess if it makes you shut the door on every other good thing in your life, like family, relationships, friendships, and other areas. Either you need to take a break and try something else or examine your motives for pursuing that dream and decide if it's time to walk away from that dream completely.

As much as I believe we can make what we desire happen when we do the right things, a massive part of making extraordinary and fulfilling things happen is recognizing when to let go of the things that no longer serve you.

In 2014, I came across a job posting that perfectly fit my skill set. I excitedly showed a co-worker, and they agreed that it was a job made for me and that I should apply. I did and got a call for an interview. I was at my best during the interview and became one of the two people out of fifteen invited for a second round of interviews.

At that point, I was almost sure I would get the job, but unfortunately, I didn't pass the second round of interviews. I asked that they keep my resumé on file just in case, although I knew the chances were slim because it was a big company.

Three years later, I saw the same position in the same department at the company and applied again. I contacted the hiring manager this time because I had the "what do I have to lose?" mentality.

The worst thing that could happen was me not getting the job, which had already happened when I was so close, and the best thing would be me getting the job. I was very willing to take my chances. And, this time, it paid off.

After two rounds of interviews and seven years of waiting, I was back in the entertainment industry.

Trying again is hard, and waiting is tough, too. Dealing with thoughts that make you think it might never happen and that your efforts are in vain is real, and it makes the journey even harder. But I have learned that these thoughts and the hardness of waiting should never lead to fear.

Don't be afraid to try again because it didn't work the first ten times. Don't be scared to take the chance because you already failed in the past. Because here's a secret. A huge part of making it happen is learning to wait and preparing like you will undoubtedly get it, even when you don't know.

Chapter 10
A Second Chance

I walked into my new company that day with a sense of peace. I was happy to be there but not overly excited. Instead of overwhelming excitement, there was a sense of assurance. I was sure I could handle whatever I was assigned, and I would devote myself to learning as I had always done for the ones I couldn't immediately handle.

I was also sure that the entertainment industry was fortunate to have me because I would add value and creativity to every task, project, and person I met on the job. It was where I had always dreamed of being, but I had come so prepared that what had been my dream would evolve and thrive simply because I was there.

It's always been weird to me how looking back, you are grateful for every road you have taken because, if you take the time to notice, it always seems like everything you have been through has prepared you for the very moment you always looked forward to—even to the minute detail.

3 The Hard Way

I have a quiet confidence now. I knew that no matter what came my way, I would have the strength and intelligence to come out of it on the other side thriving. I wasn't scared of being myself or putting my foot down to ensure I was treated with value and respect because I did not fear losing at anything. My motto was, "Put my very best into everything, and if I lost it, then it probably isn't for me."

Life is like a game. When you pass the current level, the next level opens, and what do you know? In the next level, you get to use all the skills and strength you built while trying to pass the past level. Viewing life this way gives some clarity even when we walk through our darkest moments. It also helps us not to hold on to things that do not recognize our value because we know that as long as we stay true to the journey, we will surely get to the finish line (however we choose to define what that is.)

My experiences have taught me how to deal with all types of personalities, which is a huge asset in the entertainment industry. They have also increased my patience and decision-making skills and helped me have high expectations. They've also made me open to learning, unlearning, and relearning the things I thought I knew because I've learned from all I have been through that I do not know as much as I think I know, and there's always something to learn.

I currently work in an ever-changing environment for a Global Entertainment Company on the Business and Legal Affairs team.

My duties involve reviewing TV and digital content to ensure all the images and footage are approved for airing. This requires deep observation and analysis skills to determine potential risks within the content to ensure that no legal claims arise.

A full circle moment for me was realizing that the company I had been laid off from years ago would have become a part of my company via a merger. I'm unsure what life was trying to convey by pulling that, but kudos, anyway. I have realized there's no moment where your life is ever truly over, even though it feels that way. There's nothing worth losing yourself over because even the things you think you lost forever find their way back to you, and if they do not, they are not for you, so why lose yourself over them?

Amazingly, my parents were right. The fact that I had three fingers didn't define me or my future. It was just how God had made me, and as long as I never believed anything that tried to tell me I would always be less because of my hand, I could always surmount every challenge.

I never try to hide my hand anymore. Instead, I look forward to the times when people ask me about it so I can use it as a chance to educate, inspire, or tell them they can make it happen, too. I am also part of a team that has pioneered an Employee Resource Group for Disability in the hopes that we can create an accessible work environment, help others understand disabilities, and help those who are disabled to know they are not alone and adjust seamlessly to the work environment.

3 The Hard Way

I am truly grateful for all the opportunities that life has given me. While I might not want to repeat the bad stuff, I am grateful that I can see meaning in them and see how they have prepared me to take better advantage of other opportunities. I am also thankful for my parents because they taught me to make the most of every opportunity and apply myself through hard work and perseverance until the results came.

On a trip to Dubai, I saw a sculpture that closely resembled my hand known as the Three-Fingered Salute. The salute was created by Sheikh Mohammed bin Rashid al Maktoum which represents Win, Victory, and Love and symbolizes work ethic, success and love of the nation. The statue's base serves as a reminder of what the Dubai royals wanted every human to remember that "Quality is not merely an end; it is a way of life." That definitely resonated with me personally.

Applying it to the intersection of your dreams and the realities of life would mean that the highest point you desire to reach (your dreams) isn't just a destination but the culmination of every single day of your life. So, what are you doing every day? Are you already living your dream life today? Because to make dreams happen, you must learn to exude the qualities that show you believe they are already present and just need a bit of time to manifest.

Let every day of our lives be a tale of wins and lots of love. Pursue it, and make it happen.

PART 4

BREAK A LEG, CONTINUE ANYWAY

Chapter 11
The Power Within

In Theater, performers use the expression "Break a Leg!" to wish themselves good luck. They do not want to jinx their performance, and they believe the very opposite of what they have said will come to pass. So, they say, "Break a Leg," when they really mean, "I hope you have the best performance!"

Another school of thought insists that "Break a Leg" originates from the fact that the performers have to take a bow at the end of a performance. In the process, they have to bend their knees, which they took to mean they were "breaking" a leg for their audience.

Whichever is right, they both have the same heart behind the words. They want you to have a successful performance that brings you applause and recognition. And, that is the exact sentiment I have too.

I want you to excel and thrive and have reasons to celebrate while living a fulfilling life. Even though you might break a leg (face setbacks) in the process of life, I hope you have the strength and will to continue anyway. We have more power within us than we give ourselves credit for, and I truly hope you find a reason in this book to keep trying until the things you hope for manifest.

I have learned many things from my family, friendships, the people I admire, and my life experiences. If I were to summarize them, I would call them the hacks to making your dreams happen.

Your dreams are more than what you wish for or daydream about. They are usually compelling goals, visions, and achievements you greatly desire. They resonate deeply within you, and you might feel out of place when they do not manifest. They satisfy you greatly, making you feel at peace with yourself.

Dreams aren't only related to career goals. They could also be visions of yourself building a family or helping a specific set of people. We are all different, and our dreams differ too. However, the one thing that is commonplace with any dream is the fact that there will be obstacles that try to deter you from attaining these dreams you have.

To overcome these obstacles and persevere until achievement, keep these nine things in mind.

1. Never Settle

The first obstacle to achieving your dreams is the temptation to settle for something less, which everyone else tries to convince you to be content with. You should always be content, but it is possible to be content and own the fact that you want more.

Resist the temptation to settle or convince yourself that you can make do with crumbs when, if you persevere, the whole table could be yours. But to do this, you have to know what you want. Define what you envision, who you are, and the goals and objectives you hope to attain.

If your dreams aren't defined and you're not exactly sure what you want, rejecting the lesser option becomes challenging. That is because if you aren't defining them, you cannot recognize them, and if you can't recognize them, you will probably accept anything given to you.

To settle means to live way below your potential, and it is one of the worst things that can ever happen to a human. You're also settling if you accept other people's definition of you instead of what feels authentic to you. For example, if you are the most beautiful person in your town, and everyone begins to dream that you could be the next biggest model or most famous actress, and you accept it even though what feels true to you is to be a mom or the next biggest name in science, it's still settling.

The fact that other people's dreams for you seem more glamorous or "sensible" doesn't make them yours. Your dreams need to be true to what you really desire. So, make an effort to know who you are and what you want and walk that path.

2. Never Be Afraid To Try

A secret about life is that it favors the bold, provides more light to the intentional, and lifts the seekers. So, you cannot afford to be timid or stay in a corner expecting what you want to find you. You have to put your toes in the water and then dive in if necessary.

To be bold means to be willing to try. It also means putting your all into going after what you want instead of letting the fear of "what if" hold you back from trying. It means being willing to be thrown out the door as long as you get to put your feet in. It means doing what you have to do for the life you want to live. It means not taking "no" for an answer and using your left hand if your right hand won't work. It means finding a way even when everybody else believes there's no way.

To be intentional means to live with a purpose in mind. It means everything you do leads you to where you want to be. It means not being haphazard but willing to sift out and walk away from the things that do not serve you while pursuing the things that do. It means looking beyond now, even while living fully in the present. It means knowing where you're going and taking steps every day that lead you there, much like the athlete who wants to win a medal trains every day because he knows that each day he trains compounds to prepare him for the competition.

To seek means finding the path that leads you where you want to go. It means not stopping if you don't find it on your first, second, or tenth try. It means keeping your eyes open so you do not miss the opportunities when they come.

The truth is, we never know exactly where we're going, so it is impossible to define the entire trajectory of our lives. However, life tends to drop hints that help guide us. So, while you might not know the exact career you want to be in, you do know that you want to excel at it, so what that tells you is that you must be excellent at whatever you find yourself doing.

3. Be Patient With The Process

The biggest reason people stop trying to achieve their goals is because the process is complex, long, and tiring. It's hard to put in all the effort and fail. It's hard to be laughed out of a class or a meeting because of something you were born with or are still learning to apply. It's hard to have to wait for something you are sure you are qualified for. Imagine feeling qualified for something only for life to send you another test. That can be frustrating.

However, the truth is we are not often as ready as we think we are. And, even when we are, sometimes, no matter what we do, we can't force what we want to come our way in our timing. So, we are left with no choice but to wait it out.

In these times, we must learn to build our patience muscles in the understanding that what will come will come, but in its timing. It is also vital that during our waiting periods, we surround ourselves with resources that fuel our growth and prepare us for what we are waiting for. Take that class, build those friendships, volunteer and make an impact, learn new things, etc.

Ensure you're building during the waiting period to be ready when the opportunities come.

4. Your Life Will Change - Embrace The Unexpected.

An unwritten rule in life's journey is that there will be many unexpected occurrences. There will be things you did not plan for—both good and bad things—and things that leave you wondering why or what is happening.

Sometimes, these things might not necessarily be bad or good; they just catch you unaware and leave you wondering what to do. How you handle these things might make them your best opportunities or worst nightmares.

Don't fight change. It's one thing that will remain constant throughout your life, and sometimes, changes signal growth. For example, losing a friendship you've had since childhood might hurt badly, but it might also be necessary to make certain choices that set you on the right path.

Embrace change and make the most of it. When faced with the bad stuff, it's okay to cry and be angry in the moment, but after that, open your mind to see that it is possible to fight your way out of the despair and move towards healing.

As tempting as it can be to give up when the unexpected happens, remember that any decision you make affects you. If you give up, you have to face the consequences, and if you decide to start again and push forward, you reap the benefits.

5. Do Not Wait For Everything To Be In Place Before You Make A Move

Having three fingers already meant I would never have everything that was deemed necessary for life, and I sometimes wonder what I would have become if I hadn't had parents who told me that it didn't matter what I didn't have, I could use what I did have to achieve everything I wanted.

Sometimes, we go through the waiting seasons because we are waiting for everything to be perfect before we make a move. Instead of looking towards what we can achieve with what we have, we focus on what we do not have and why what we want to achieve is impossible because we aren't ready.

We'll never feel completely ready, so why not move towards what we desire? Of course, this doesn't mean certain things don't need to be in place before we place demands, but we must learn to differentiate between the significant things and the other things.

For example, if you desire to be a doctor, you need a doctor's license—a significant requirement. However, if you refuse to apply for any jobs or internships until you perfect your skills, you are trying to wait for perfect conditions before you start. And, if you think about it, how will you perfect your skills if you do not have someone to guide you and all that's obtainable at a job?

It might seem nice to try to wait for perfect conditions, and you might even have excellent reasons to back it up, but the truth is you need to make that move already.

6. Be Alert. Your Deepest Lessons and Opportunities Might Come From A Stranger.

This is a lesson in being observant and open to experiences and people. The solutions you seek will not always come to you in the way you expect. For example, you might get an answer to a question you've had for a long time from a one-time conversation with someone you helped at the bus stop.

You might get an opportunity because the stranger on the bus with whom you exchanged pleasantries turned out to be on the panel reviewing your proposal. Life doesn't come with a handbook. Weird things are going to happen. Learn to soak up your experiences.

This is also a lesson in networking. Reach out to people. It's okay to make the first move, too. Be friendly, be curious about others, and genuinely have a heart for the other person. The purpose isn't to get something in return but to be the reason another human smiled or had an interesting day.

7. Don't Be Afraid To Fail

Success leaves a trail behind it, and surprisingly, this trail doesn't always have medals and proof of other successful moments. Instead, it usually testifies to how many times the person tried and failed, tried and failed again, and probably again until he succeeded.

So, it's okay to fail as long as you understand that the reason for failure is to learn one way not to do it or to know what to tweak to achieve what you seek. Failure isn't something to be ashamed of, so do not allow yourself to hide your head in shame because you failed.

Instead, let failure be a catalyst for growth. Let it be the reason you try again, and the reason you discover a better way to do that thing.

8. Rest, But Don't Quit.

We do not often hear that it is okay to rest and take a break. But it is. It's okay to rest when things are overwhelming, and you need to clear your head. Take a break. Do something entirely different if you have to.

Sometimes, we lose passion for our dreams because we've immersed ourselves so much in them that we lose the will to continue to pursue them. This is a classic case of sugar becoming undesirable because we have too much of it. So, take a break.

Make time to focus on the other parts of your life, too. Fulfillment from other aspects of your life can give you more fuel to keep pursuing a goal. You need that fuel for strength to make your dreams happen.

It is also critical to understand that your dream should encompass every area of your life. Its achievement should find you healthy, mentally stable, loved, and financially buoyant, among other things, instead of focusing on one area of your life.

When things get tough, don't feel guilty that you can't do as much as you used to. Just take the time to rest, get better, and then get back to it.

9. Be Ready To Receive - Prepare

Your dreams are possible. As you go through life and its experiences, opportunities will be made available to you. The only way to turn those opportunities into the manifestation of your dreams is to recognize them and then maximize them.

Unfortunately, you cannot recognize or maximize something you are unprepared for. For example, an opening for a legal position in an entertainment company only made sense to me because I had prepared for it by becoming a paralegal (that is recognition).

I excelled at my job so much that I was trusted with things beyond the typical tasks. This was only possible because I had learned patience, observation, and social interaction, preparing me to maximize what I had received.

The truth is, if you approach an opportunity unprepared, you're most likely to lose it. So, always be ready to receive what you desire by preparing ahead. Remember, life has a way of bringing you tests that equip you with the tools you need for your future; all you need to do is learn.

Chapter 12
You Can Make It Happen

Dear Reader,

It's been a pleasure sharing my stories with you. I hope they resonate and give you some answers to questions you've always had.

I firmly believe that possibilities abound if we only stay long enough and put in the effort and faith required to achieve the great things we desire.

I know how hard it is to look beyond the present into what is possible. Sometimes, we only have enough strength to make it to the next day—and that's okay. I hope you remember that even though all you can see in the present is darkness, there's light just beyond it. I hope you remember that you're not less because of the things you do not have.

You have so much within you that the world needs and it would be sad if they never saw the light of day. Life throws challenges at everyone. There will be times when you stumble, when doubt creeps in, and when giving up seems like the easiest option. But here's the truth – we all have a choice. We can let these obstacles define us or use them to become stronger and more resilient versions of ourselves.

Just like me, you can choose to tackle life head-on. Develop a growth mindset. Believe that you can learn and improve, no matter what life throws your way. Take small steps – no matter how small, every victory is a step closer to your dreams.

Now, it's your turn. What dreams have been waiting on the sidelines? Don't let fear or doubt hold you back anymore. Write those dreams down. Create a plan of action, no matter how simple it may seem, and take the first step today.

The path might not be smooth sailing. There will be bumps and detours, moments when you want to throw in the towel. But remember, you are not alone. Draw strength from those who believe in you, and most importantly, believe in yourself. You have the power to overcome any obstacle and achieve anything you set your mind to. The possibilities are truly endless.

Also, take a moment to celebrate your progress and acknowledge how far you've come. You've overcome obstacles, learned from experiences, and grown. Be proud of yourself.

This concludes our journey together, dear reader. But remember, the most incredible stories are the ones we write ourselves. Go forth, courageously embrace life's challenges, and make your dreams a reality. You can MAKE IT HAPPEN!!!

Acknowledgements:

This book is dedicated to first and foremost God for giving me life, the strength and time to write this book that I continually put off.

Secondly, I dedicated this book to my Grandmother and other ancestors who paved the way for my family and I. Speaking of family, this book is dedicated to my parents; for without them, I wouldn't be alive but especially to my Mom who's always has led me down the right path and instilled me with the knowledge to always do the right thing. This book also is dedicated to my brother Jonathan who is also an author, who always has given me encouragement as well as different perspectives, insight and new ideas.

I'd also like to dedicate the book to my aunts Carol, Beverly and Valerie (who recently passed away in 2023…R.I.H.) who have ALWAYS prayed for and supported me throughout my journey in life. Huge shout out to my older cousins letting me hang around them when I was younger and further develop my love of music.

To all my friends who pushed me forward or has ever helped me out. For those who have given me a ride when I wasn't able to drive, to anyone who has brought me a drink or dinner and celebrated with me; to the people that gave me their time whether it was listening to me or keeping me company during trying times and giving me encouragement to fight another day; to those who never judged me and accepted me for who I am and what I have. I promise you, you will forever be in my heart.

www.ingramcontent.com/pod-product-compliance
Lightning Source LLC
Chambersburg PA
CBHW020309010526
44107CB00001B/34